I0750260

# Biblical Mothers Of Distinction

*by Walter G. Lofton*

**Published by Escarpment Press**

Biblical Mothers of Distinction

ISBN: 978-1-7346750-8-5



10 9 8 7 6 5 4 3 2 1

# CONTENTS

# Biblical Mothers Of Distinction

By

Walter Lofton

## Foreword

It is my humble pleasure to present to you this volume about outstanding mothers of the Bible. Each of these mothers had her personal moments of sorrow and grief as well as triumphs and joy. Some of these mothers are well known, while others are somewhat obscure. However, each of them was used by God for a special purpose that He had providentially ordained. Each one performed her role admirably as she walked through the pages of history and left us a profile of encouragement and faith.

All Scriptural references in this volume are taken from the Authorized Version of 1611 Bible, more commonly known as the King James Version.

As I review the lives of these and other godly mothers, I cannot help but think of my own godly mother that God so graciously allowed me to have. She was devout in her love and devotion to God long before I was born. Her love and guiding influence in my life is worth more than all the world's gold. She went to her heavenly reward one day before my thirtieth birthday. I look forward to joining her when I receive my summons from the Heavenly Father.

I would like to share one beautiful memory that I cherish concerning my mother. After I left home, I would visit on weekends once or twice a month. On one such visit I was sleeping late while Mother prepared breakfast. In the middle of her cooking, she came into my room and sat on the side of my bed with her apron to her eyes and said: "Walter, you are my joy. I love you." She immediately wiped her eyes and returned to the kitchen to finish preparing breakfast. This warmed my heart and I have never forgotten this spontaneous expression of my mother's devoted love. It is to her love and memory that I dedicate this book.

Walter Lofton

# Eve

## *The Mother of All Living*

*"And Adam called his wife's name Eve; because she was the mother of all living."* (Genesis 3:20)

It is fitting to begin this book on Bible mothers with Eve who was the very first mother on Earth, making her the mother of the human race. There is not a whole lot said about Eve in the scriptures, but enough is said of her to give us a glimpse of her uniqueness on the stage of human existence. To see her as God would have us see her, we must begin at the beginning just as God did in His infallible Word. By necessity we must first take a look at her husband, Adam, to see how Eve fits into the overall picture.

The first biblical record of mankind's existence on earth is found in Genesis chapter one, verses 26 and 27. *"And God said, Let us make man in our image, after our likeness: and let them have dominion over the fish of the sea, and over the fowl of the air, and over the cattle, and over all the earth, and over every creeping thing that creepeth upon the earth.* (27) *So God created man in his own image, in the image of God created he him; male and female created he them."*

A word of explanation is perhaps in order concerning the biblical terminology that is used here. Notice the words "man" and "them" in these verses of Scripture. Both of these words refer to mankind or the human race in general. In scriptural references to members of the human race, including both the male and the female, one can see the words "man" or "mankind" being used. In the above verses one can see that both male and female are meant by the term "man."

In today's "politically correct" society, many seem to be offended when their pet (or narrow and biased) verbiage is not used. For example, I was listening to the news one evening when a woman from our neighboring country of Canada was giving a report and she innocently used the word "mankind." She was stopped by that country's president who suggested that she change that word to "peoplekind." I suppose there is nothing wrong with using that particular word to denote one of the human race, but to me the word "humankind" would be a better word if indeed she must change it to appease the "elitist" in the crowd. Biblical terminology often runs afoul of today's modern culture. Since this is a book about Bible mothers, we will use biblical terminology and trust that those who may differ with our language will understand and bear with us inasmuch as we do not aim to offend. So much for the explanation on terminology, now let us get on with our insight into our universal mother, Eve.

God formed Adam from the dust of the ground and breathed into his nostrils the breath of life, and Adam became a living soul. His (and our) life literally came from the breath of God. God went on to say: *"It is not good that the man should be alone; I will make him an help meet for him"* (Genesis 2:18).

The word "meet" here means suitable. Therefore "help meet" means a suitable helper. Scripture goes on to say: *"And the LORD God caused a deep sleep to fall upon*

*Adam, and he slept: and he took one of his ribs, and closed up the flesh instead thereof;)* (22) *And the rib, which the LORD God had taken from man, made he a woman, and brought her unto the man.* (23) *And Adam said, This is now bone of my bones, and flesh of my flesh: she shall be called Woman, because she was taken out of Man.* (24) *Therefore shall a man leave his father and his mother, and shall cleave unto his wife: and they shall be one flesh"* (Genesis 2:21-24).

Notice that Adam called his help meet "woman" which referred to **what** she was rather than **who** she was. She was to be called "woman" indicating the gender of the human race that she represented. It was not until verse twenty of chapter three of Genesis that she is given a personal name, "Eve," indicating who or which woman she was. And so it has been from that time on with each one of us to distinguish our individual being from all other human beings on the face of the earth.

For a little background information let's look at the following verses. *"And the LORD God planted a garden eastward in Eden; and there he put the man whom he had formed.* (Genesis 2:8). In verse 9, Scripture says: *"And out of the ground made the LORD God to grow every tree that is pleasant to the sight, and good for food; the tree of life also in the midst of the garden, and the tree of knowledge of good and evil."* Further instructions are given to the man in verses 16 and 17. *"And the LORD God commanded the man, saying, Of every tree of the garden thou mayest freely eat:* (17) *But of the tree of the knowledge of good and evil, thou shalt not eat of it: for in the day that thou eatest thereof thou shalt surely die."* In the last verse of chapter two we read:

*"And they were both naked, the man and his wife, and were not ashamed."*

Notice that these instructions were given to Adam before God formed Eve from one of his ribs. It would become Adam's responsibility to teach his future wife the commands of God. The Word of God places the headship of the wife, family and children upon the husband and father figure in the home. See Ephesians 5:23 and other scriptures on this matter. *"For the husband is the head of the wife, even as Christ is the head of the church: and he is the saviour of the body."* This verse of scripture relates a much deeper meaning and honor to all wives and especially one special honor to Eve alone.

The husband-and-wife relationship to each other is a spiritual reflection of the relationship between Christ and His bride-to-be, the Church. In addressing the husband-and-wife relationship the Apostle Paul says in Ephesians 5:31 and 32: *"For this cause shall a man leave his father and mother, and shall be joined unto his wife, and they two shall be one flesh.* (32*) This is a great mystery: but I speak concerning Christ and the church."* Eve, being the first wife and Adam, being the first husband represented a reflection (which the scriptures depict as a type and shadow) of a much more profound lesson of God to mankind, being that of Christ and His Bride, the Church. Therefore Adam, being the first man and husband that God created became a symbol of Christ and Eve, the first woman and wife became a symbol of the Church. What a beautiful honor bestowed upon Eve, the world's very first wife!

God created mankind with a will and gave him the right to exercise this will by making his own choices in life. He made mankind in this manner because His overall purpose in the creation was to have a being that would voluntarily worship and obey Him out of choice rather than force (see Revelation 4:12). Therefore, there must by necessity be something from which to choose. That is why God instructed the man not to eat of the tree of the knowledge of good and evil.

Somewhere along the way Satan was cast out of Heaven to the earth. He was here ready to tempt man to make the wrong choice against God's will. The contest was not between Adam and the trees, but between God and Satan. The reason the trees were there was because man was a physical being and would need physical objects to choose between. Satan and God, both being spiritual beings could not be seen nor touched by Adam.

Now let's look a little deeper into the character of Eve. I will assume that most of my readers are familiar with holy Scripture. Therefore, I will not be as detailed with most of my dialogue as I would be to someone whom I knew did not know anything at all about the Bible.

After the creation of Adam and Eve, God placed them into the garden He had made where they were obliged to "live happily ever after," but that did not happen. Lurking nearby was the master deceiver Satan, their second choice of allegiance, who was also allowed in the garden by God in order to give them the option of choice.

The scriptures tell it like this in Genesis 3:1-7: "*Now the serpent was more subtil than any beast of the field which the LORD God had made. And he said unto the woman, Yea, hath God said, Ye shall not eat of every tree of the garden?* (2) *And the woman said unto the serpent, We may eat of the fruit of the trees of the garden:* (3) *But of the fruit of the tree which is in the midst of the garden, God hath said, Ye shall not eat of it, neither shall ye touch it, lest ye die.* (4) *And the serpent said unto the woman, Ye shall not surely die:* (5) *For God doth know that in the day ye eat thereof, then your eyes shall be opened, and ye shall be as gods, knowing good and evil.* (6) *And when the woman saw that the tree was good for food, and that it was pleasant to the eyes, and a tree to be desired to make one wise, she took of the fruit thereof, and did eat, and gave also unto her husband with her; and he did eat.* (7) *And the eyes of them both were opened, and they knew that they were naked; and they sewed fig leaves together, and made themselves aprons.*

We find in these verses of Scripture several key points that help us see the overall picture being painted by God. We see Satan coming to the woman in the form of the serpent. The form of the serpent was used to indicate the craftiness being used against the clear thinking of the woman. Instead of stating the fact of God's instructions he turned it into a question. Satan still employs that tactic on us today trying to get us to doubt God's Word instead of taking it at face value by faith.

When Satan turned the tables on Eve in this manner her clear thinking became clouded. Her answer started out just fine but ended up in deception, which was cleverly designed by her tempter to cause her downfall. Her reply ended with *"neither shall ye touch it."* God did not say not to touch it for he had already given Adam the responsibility of dressing (pruning) and keeping the garden in tip-top shape. They must therefore touch it in order to fulfill this command of God.

When we change or misinterpret the Word of God, we open ourselves up to losing connection to our relationship with God either innocently or deliberately. When this happens, we are in danger of being eternally lost. The Apostle Paul in the New Testament warns us of this danger in Second Corinthians 11:3 *"But I fear, lest by any means, as the serpent beguiled Eve through his subtilty, so your minds should be corrupted from the simplicity that is in Christ."*

Satan responded to Eve by stating that she would surely not die but rather would come to know good and evil. This appealed to Eve and she put forth her hand and took the fruit and ate it and then offered it to her husband Adam and he ate of it also. This is where sin entered the human race. This act of Adam and Eve was the very first sin to be committed upon the earth. Immediately their (spiritual). eyes were opened and they saw that they were naked and they were ashamed. Sin causes shame, remorse, disgrace, guilt and regret upon the human race. Christ came to save us from our sin and shame and bring us back into the right relationship with God, our Creator.

Christ's future coming to save us from our sins was promised in Genesis 3:15. *"And I will put enmity between thee and the woman, and between thy seed and her seed; it shall bruise thy head, and thou shalt bruise his heel."* This was a prophecy of the coming of Christ to be the supreme sacrifice for the sins of all mankind who would choose to believe on Him according to the famous verse of Scripture found in John 3:16. *"For God so loved the world, that he gave his only begotten Son, that whosoever believeth in him should not perish, but have everlasting life."*

This seed (offspring) of the woman was a prophetic reference to Christ who was born of the Virgin Mary as the Son of God. As by one man, (Adam) sin entered into the world also by one Man (Christ) the world would be able to be free from the condemnation of sin (see Romans, chapter 5). This blessed mother Mary, the chosen mother of Christ, will be featured near the end of this book.

The story continues with their being driven out of the garden to fend for themselves in a lifetime of sorrow and regret. It was in this condition that their first two sons were born. The scriptures do not give details about all their offspring but considering the fact that Adam lived to be 930 years of age one must conclude that they must have had perhaps hundreds of children. The first son, Cain, killed his innocent brother, Abel. After this God gave them another son who was called Seth, which means one appointed by God. Seth had a son he called Enos. After Enos was born people began to call on the name of the Lord.

In reading this scriptural account of our first earthly father and mother and considering other scriptures we are led to think and perhaps believe that Adam and Eve must have surely taught their offspring about God and

His will for the human race. How else would their second son, Abel be counted as righteous in God's sight and their third son, Seth and his son, Enos know that they should acknowledge God in their daily affairs?

I believe we can give credit to Eve, our first mother and Adam, our first father for guiding their children's pathway toward God. Perhaps also they may have repented and found favor in God's sight. We do not really know for sure, but we sincerely hope so.

# Sarah

## *A Mother of Promise*

*"And God said, Sarah thy wife shall bear thee a son indeed; and thou shalt call his name Isaac: and I will establish my covenant with him for an everlasting covenant, and with his seed after him."* (Genesis 17:19)

Sarah was the wife of Abraham who is known as the father of the faithful and a friend of God. Abraham whose name originally was called Abram was the son of Terah of Ur in the land of the Chaldees.

Terah took Abraham and his wife, Sarai (her name was later changed to Sarah) and Lot, Abraham's nephew and set out for the land of Canaan. Before reaching Canaan, they stopped over in Haran (present day Iran) and while there, Terah died being 205 years old.

Afterwards God spoke to Abraham and directed him to go to a land that He would show him which is later identified in the scriptures to be the land of Canaan. As a condition of his obedience God promised to make him a great nation and bless all the families of the earth through him.

These promises were significant for two main reasons. First, this meant that Sarah, whose name means "princess" would become a mother. Of course, this was necessary in order for Abraham's descendants to become a great nation. But this was impossible because Sarah was unable to have children because she was barren. It required faith on their part to believe and accept such a phenomenal promise. At first Sarah doubted. During an angelic visitation to Abraham and Sarah with the announcement of the fulfillment of God's promise that she would bear Abraham a son she laughed in doubt. But Abraham believed God against all odds according to Romans 4:18-21. *"Who against hope believed in hope, that he might become the father of many nations, according to that which was spoken, So shall thy seed be.* (19) *And being not weak in faith, he considered not his own body now dead, when he was about an hundred years old, neither yet the deadness of Sara's womb:* (20) *He staggered not at the promise of God through unbelief; but was strong in faith, giving glory to God;* (21) *And being fully persuaded that, what he had promised, he was able also to perform."*

The second and most important reason for this promise of a child was that through the bloodline of Abraham God would send His Son into the world to bear the sins of all mankind. Therefore, through the offspring of Sarah would be the beginning of the generations that would eventually lead to the birth of Christ.

The life of Sarah would take some twists and turns before the eventual fulfillment of this promise. Her doubting heart would have to be transformed into a believing heart. In this process of her change of heart her life would experience some up and downs with disappointments and unnecessary grief. The end results would be glorious and the world would be forever changed for the better.

After the death of his father, Abraham came into the land of Canaan. He came unto the plain of Moreh, and the Lord appeared unto him and told him that this land would become the land of his descendants. From there he went to a place called Bethel, and after this he went toward the south. When a famine arose in the land, Abraham journeyed into Egypt. While there, Sarah was stolen away and brought before Pharaoh.

When they entered Egypt, Abraham instructed Sarah to say she was his sister instead of his wife. The reason for this was that she was a beautiful woman (with a princess-like persona) and he feared that the people would kill him and take her away. It was not entirely untrue that Sarah was Abraham's sister for she was his half-sister and his wife.

God began to send plagues upon the house of Pharaoh because Sarah' being taken there frustrated the purpose of God. When Pharaoh found out that she was indeed the wife of Abraham he became fearful and returned her unto Abraham.

There was strife between the herdsmen of Abraham and Lot. They separated with Lot choosing the luscious plains with his herds and Abraham taking the rough mountain for his herds. While dwelling in the plains, Lot was tempted to move on into the city of Sodom. God saw the wickedness of Sodom and proposed to destroy it along with the wicked city of Gomorrah. It was at this point in time that the angels of the Lord were sent unto Abraham with the sad news.

Knowing that his nephew Lot would most likely be destroyed with these wicked cities Abraham pled with the angels not to destroy the cities. He pleaded for God not to destroy the city if there were fifty righteous persons found there. He narrowed the gap down to forty-five, then forty, then thirty, on down to twenty, and eventually to ten. Not even ten righteous people could be found there, but God did send His angels to literally take Lot, his wife, and two daughters by the hand and lead them without the city before He rained down fire from Heaven to destroy the cities. No doubt, the bargaining Abraham did with the angels of the Lord is where the term "jewing someone down" came into use. Usually when someone wants a bargain, they will keep narrowing the odds to get a better deal.

It was during this visit of the angels that the promise of a child was renewed and Sarah laughed at the impossibility saying: "*. . . After I am waxed* [or grown] *old shall I have pleasure, my lord* [husband] *being old also?* (13)" *. . . Shall I of a surety bear a child, which am old?"* (Genesis 18:12, 13). Preceding this announcement and Sarah's laugh, Scripture tells us: *"Now Abraham and Sarah were old and well stricken in age; and it ceased to be with Sarah* *after the manner of women"* (v. 11). The angels said unto Abraham, *"Is any thing too hard for the LORD? At the time appointed I will return unto thee, according to the time of life, and Sarah shall have a son"* (v. 14).

It is here at this juncture that we get a glimpse into the character of Sarah. She referred to her husband Abraham as her lord. The Apostle Peter in his writings in the New Testament refers to this in First Peter 3:6. *"Even as Sara obeyed Abraham, calling him lord: whose daughters ye are, as long as ye do well, and are not afraid with any amazement."* This shows the respect a godly wife gives to her husband which is consistent with biblical teachings. The Apostle Peter also states in verses one and two: *"Likewise, ye wives, be in subjection to your own husbands; that, if any obey not the word, they also may without the word be won by the conversation* [character or lifestyle] *of the wives;* (2) *While they behold your chaste conversation coupled with fear."*

The biblical instructions do not stop there. Life is a two-way street. Peter also addresses the husbands' responsibility in verse seven. *"Likewise, ye husbands, dwell with them according to knowledge, giving honour unto the wife, as unto the weaker vessel, and as being heirs together of the grace of life; that your prayers be not hindered."*

This subject is also addressed by the Apostle Paul. In Ephesians 5:22-24 Paul writes: *"Wives, submit yourselves unto your own husbands, as unto the Lord.* (23) *For the husband is the head of the wife, even as Christ is the head of the church: and he is the saviour of the body.* (24) *Therefore as the church is subject unto Christ, so let the wives be to their own husbands in every thing."* And he addresses the husband's responsibility in verse twenty-five: *"Husbands, love your wives, even as Christ also loved the church, and gave himself for it."* How much did Christ love the Church? HE DIED FOR HER! (See Acts 20:28). That is a lot of love! The Word of God places the wife in a very protective state. The truly godly husband will defend his wife even with his own life if necessary.

In looking into the character of Sarah we see the flaws as well as the goodness she exhibits. One of her weaknesses, as already stated, was her lack of faith. All of us are probably guilty, along with her, in this matter of faith at some point in our lives. While she found it hard to grasp the fact that she would never become a mother she settled for the next best thing. That was to become a mother by proxy. She offered her husband her maid to bear him a son. Abraham yielded to this carnal suggestion and Sarah's maid Hagar gave birth to Ishmael. Fourteen years after the birth of Ishmael, Isaac was born of Sarah just as God had promised. Sarah becoming a mother at ninety years of age, and her husband becoming a father at one hundred years of age was truly miraculous! Once more Sarah laughed. This laugh was one of joy and not of doubt as was her former laughing was. She was exuberant with joy and wanted everyone to join in with her in her celebration. Even her son's name Isaac, means laughter.

The long period of waiting was over and a divine promise that appeared impossible finally became reality. God always pays off on His promises. He does not ever fail. There is nothing impossible with Him. Sometimes it seems that He just wants to test our faith. Thank God that many can say with the patriarch Job: *"But he knoweth the way that I take: when he hath tried me, I shall come forth as gold."* (Job 23:10).

God had a divine purpose in all that He did in the lives of Abraham and Sarah. Over and over God assured Abraham that his promised offspring would be counted in the person of his son, Isaac. When Ishmael was a teen, he persecuted the young Isaac. The mother nature in Sarah said enough is enough. Drive Hagar and Ishmael away that my son, Isaac may grow up in peace. *"Wherefore she said unto Abraham, Cast out this bondwoman and her son: for the son of this bondwoman shall not be heir with my son, even with Isaac"* (Genesis 21:19). Abraham was apprehensible about this matter and God had to reassure him. God told Abraham; *"Let it not be grievous in thy sight because of the lad, and because of thy bondwoman; in all that Sarah hath said unto thee, hearken unto her voice; for in Isaac shall thy seed be called"* (Genesis 21:12).

God had told Abraham in Genesis 17:19 and 21: "*. . . Sarah thy wife shall bear thee a son indeed; and thou shalt call his name Isaac: and I will establish my covenant with him for an everlasting covenant, and with his seed after him.* (21) *But my covenant will I establish with Isaac, which Sarah shall bear unto thee at this set time in the next year."*

It was through Abraham, his son, Isaac, and Isaac's son, Jacob (later changed to Israel) that God's chosen people would come. God did bless Ishmael for Abraham' sake but Ishmael was not on God's divine program. God said of Ishmael: *"And he will be a wild man; his hand will be against every man, and every man's hand against him; and he shall dwell in the presence of all his brethren"* (Genesis 16:12). This prophecy is being played out even today in the Middle East. The Ishmaelites morphed into several modern nations, which are predominant Arab, and for the most part, embrace the Muslim religion. The terror they inflict on most of the world is a direct fulfillment of the Word of the Lord to Hagar, Ishmael's mother when they were driven out from the family of Abraham. Without doubt, these modern problems can be traced back to Sarah's weak faith.

Except for this one area in Sarah's life, she was quiet and gentle. She did not rebel against Abraham when he left their original home in Er of the Chaldees, nor when they went into Egypt, nor when Abraham and Lot separated and later on not even when God tested Abraham by asking him to take Isaac to sacrifice him for a burnt offering. This was only a test—Abraham's final test—it was not really meant to be carried out. Without her the nation of Israel could not have come into being. She was faithful to fill her place and become a mother of promise. God promised. He fulfilled. We are the benefactors. Thank God for Sarah, a mother of divine promise.

# Rebekah

## *A Mother of Thousands of Millions*

*"And they called Rebekah, and said unto her, Wilt thou go with this man? And she said, I will go."* (Genesis 24:58)

After the death of Sarah, Abraham began to consider the future of his son, Isaac. Isaac was now forty years of age and Abraham wanted to see him married while he was yet alive. Abraham had put the care of his entire household into the hands of his trusted servant, Eliezer. He called Eliezer and made him swear that he would not take a wife for his son from among the daughters of the Canaanites among whom he lived. He was instructed to go back to his kindred in his original homeland and find a wife for his son Isaac.

The servant prepared for the long trip with necessary goods and camels and set out to Mesopotamia unto the city of Nahor, the brother of Abraham. Upon arriving there he was tired and thirsty. He stopped by a well of water and prayed for God to direct him to the chosen young woman. The custom of that day provided that the women of the household would draw water from the well daily for the needs of their households. So, he stopped at a well, which was an ideal place to meet women and waited.

For assurance from God that he would not make a mistake in choosing the right woman for his master's son he asked God to give him a sign that would lead him to the right girl. The sign he prayed for was that when he asked the girl for a drink of water, she would give him a drink and volunteer to draw water for his camels as well. While he was still speaking the prayer in his heart Rebekah came to the well to draw water. She was young and beautiful. The servant meekly asked her for a drink of water. Rebekah responded and while he was sipping the water, she volunteered to draw water for his camels also.

The servant was overwhelmed but did not immediately reveal his purpose for being there. The most important criteria to seal the choice would yet need to be determined. So, he asked her in a nervous voice, *"Whose daughter art thou?"* Rebekah responded by saying that she was the daughter of Bethuel the son of Milcah, which she bare unto Nahor. Upon realizing that this young lady was of the kindred of his master Abraham, the servant bowed his head and thanked God for His providence and then presented her with gifts. In her amazed excitement she left her water pitcher and ran back home to tell her family. Her brother, Laban came out to meet the man and invited him to come to their father's house to be refreshed and rest.

Upon arriving at the house, the necessary introductions were made, and he immediately made known the purpose of his journey. He explained who he was, about Sarah being dead and Abraham commissioning him to find a wife for his son among his kindred. The story was unusual but acceptable in their sight, for the unseen hand of God was moving in their heart just as He did in the heart of Rebekah back at the well, and they agreed to let Rebekah return with him to become the wife of Abraham's son. The servant was greatly relieved and thankful and gave praise to God for directing him to the right family and prospective bride.

The servant, feeling that God had prospered his way, was ready to return back to his master Abraham with the good news and with the future bride of Isaac. The family, seeing the seriousness of the matter, was reluctant to let the girl go away with this stranger so soon. They entreated him to let her remain for about ten days longer before he took her away with him. We will let the scriptures tell this part of the story here. The reference is to Genesis 24:54-59. *"And they did eat and drink, he and the men that were with him, and tarried all night; and they rose up in the morning, and he said, Send me away unto my master.* (55) *And her brother and her mother said, Let the damsel abide with us a few days, at the least ten; after that she shall go.* (56) *And he said unto them, Hinder me not, seeing the LORD hath prospered my way; send me away that I may go to my master.* (57) *And they said, We will call the damsel, and enquire at her mouth.* (58) *And they called Rebekah, and said unto her, Wilt thou go with this man? And she said, I will go.* (59) *And they sent away Rebekah their sister, and her nurse, and Abraham's servant, and his men."*

This strange man left with their daughter and sister. They would never see her again, ever. The things that we are accustomed to today such as Facebook, cell phones, email, etc. did not exist back then, neither did the postal system that we sometimes tend to think is a little outdated. (I still rely on it and like it just fine myself.) There was just a long dusty trail to a strange unknown land that lay far away. Their beloved sister and daughter would be leaving them, never to return again. **What sweet sorrow!** So, they wanted to send her off with a blessing that would be befitting for the solemn occasion. They gave her this blessing from their hearts to hers. *"And they blessed Rebekah, and said unto her, Thou art our sister,* ***be thou the mother of thousands of millions,*** *and let thy seed possess the gate of those which hate them"* (Genesis 24:60). With this tearful send-off *"...Rebekah arose, and her damsels, and they rode upon the camels, and followed the man: and the servant took Rebekah, and went his way."*

Now let us turn our attention to the anticipation and thoughts of a young man's lonely heart that was several hundred miles away. *"And Isaac came from the way of the well Lahairoi; for he dwelt in the south country.* (v. 62) *And Isaac went out to meditate in the field at the eventide: and he lifted up his eyes, and saw, and, behold, the camels were coming"* (v. 63).

A long and laborious journey was nearing an end. It had been several long days, even weeks, when the camel train set out on its unique mission. No doubt, Isaac went out into this field each day and gazed at the distant horizon for the hopeful sight of some movement that he might interpret as a group of camels approaching in his direction. On this particular day, he was tired. His heart ached with a mixture of hope and doubt. He had gone out each day and nothing happened. Would this be just another long uneventful day? Would this day prolong his agony of waiting for fulfillment, or perhaps disappointment? He could not know for sure but he faithfully waited and watched and hoped. Then it happened. At first, he thought he caught a glimpse of a dust cloud on the horizon. *Is it – could it – Oh, God, let it be them!* He watched with great anticipation. He strained his eyes so as not to miss one second of the scene before them. Was it—it sure looked like it—yes, it was indeed a train of camels. Yes, the camels were coming!

As they came closer, his heart skipped a beat. His palms became sweaty. His eyes were blurred. *Did they find her? Did she come with them? Was she beautiful? Would she love him? Would she be anything like his dear mother, Sarah?*

The camel train drew closer and Rebekah could discern the lone figure of a man in the distance. Her heart was also beating fast. Her mind was spinning as she wondered what the next few minutes would reveal. Was this the man she was coming to marry? What if he did not approve of her, what then? She could not return for she knew not the way and could never survive such a long journey alone. What lay ahead in her future? As her heart was pondering these thoughts, she asked the servant, *"What man is this that walketh in the field to meet us?"* the servant replied, *"It is my master."* She then took a veil and covered herself as was the custom in those days. Then she lighted off the camel and went to meet her Isaac. *"And the servant told Isaac all things that he had done* (v. 66) *And Isaac brought her into his mother Sarah's tent, and took Rebekah, and she became his wife;* ***and he loved her: and Isaac was comforted after his mother's death"*** (v. 67).

Now for a little character analysis of our subject, Rebekah, the projected mother of thousands of millions. She was young. She was beautiful. She was a dependable and faithful daughter in that she performed her domestic duties admirably. These were her natural qualities. Her spiritual qualities were even better. Her spirit was yielded to the pull of God's Spirit. Her heart was pure in discerning rightful motives. Her mind was sharp enough to grasp an understanding of circumstances. Her soul was brave enough to trust the things she felt, saw, and could understand. She was from the specified family lineage. She passed the test the servant laid out in his prayer to God. The big question that loomed was would she be willing to believe this man's story and go with him? History tells us that indeed she did.

After she became the appointed wife of Isaac, she found that she was barren. Genesis 25:21-28 gives us the narrative. *"And Isaac intreated the LORD for his wife, because she was barren: and the LORD was intreated of him, and Rebekah his wife conceived.* (22) *And the children struggled together within her; and she said, If it be so, why am*

*I thus? And she went to enquire of the LORD.* (23) *And the LORD said unto her, Two nations are in thy womb, and two manner of people shall be separated from thy bowels; and the one people shall be stronger than the other people; and the elder shall serve the younger.* (24) *And when her days to be delivered were fulfilled, behold, there were twins in her womb* (25) *And the first came out red, all over like an hairy garment; and they called his name Esau.* (26) *And after that came his brother out, and his hand took hold on Esau's heel; and his name was called Jacob: and Isaac was threescore years old when she bare them.* (27) *And the boys grew: and Esau was a cunning hunter, a man of the field; and Jacob was a plain man, dwelling in tents.* (28) *And Isaac loved Esau, because he did eat of his venison: but Rebekah loved Jacob."*

Isaac's bride Rebekah, the projected "mother of thousands of millions" was found to be barren, which meant that she could not become the mother of even one child. This situation prevailed for twenty long years. Isaac prayed to God for his wife and God heard and answered his prayer and Rebekah conceived and bore not only one child, but twins! When God answers prayer, He answers big! The above scripture tells us that "Isaac was threescore years old" when their twin boys were born. A score equals twenty years and Isaac was already forty years old when he and Rebekah were married. This means that he was sixty years old when the children were born.

Isaac was born of a miraculous birth himself, for Abraham prayed to God for a son after both he and his wife Sarah were old and past the age of childbearing. Now a similar situation existed inasmuch as Rebekah was barren. Bear in mind that God promised Abraham that his offspring would be innumerable, even as the stars of heaven and the sand of the earth in number. In the book of Romans in chapter 4, verse 18, we are told this of Abraham: *"Who against hope believed in hope, that he might become the father of many nations, according to that which was spoken, So shall thy seed be."*

Isn't it amazing how God sets up problems in our lives that are impossible for us to solve and then teaches us to wait expectantly on Him in faith as He sends a miracle to solve the problems? Abraham believed God's promise against impossible odds, and it seems that his son, Isaac, did also. Like father, like son definitely applied here!

As time wore on in the lives of these sons and they became grown up, a definite trend had developed in the hearts of their parents. (Such is the case in most families of today as well.) The Scripture tells us that: ". . . *Isaac loved Esau, because he did eat of his venison: but Rebekah loved Jacob."* This was not a problem apparently until the time came for the traditional blessing of the "birthright" to be administered. The birthright was a granting to the first-born son a double portion of the family inheritance and the authority to administer the governing rule and priestly duties to the family clan at the death of the father. Esau was considered the eldest son because he was born first. Technically speaking they were both the same age. The father served as the priest of the family and this was considered a high honor to the one receiving it.

When Isaac grew old and nearly blind, he called for his older son, Esau to go into the field to hunt for some venison and prepare it for him. Remember, Isaac preferred Esau because he liked to eat of his venison. Esau knew just how to fix it for his father's pleasure. At the end of this feast Isaac was preparing to bless Esau with the blessing of the birthright.

Rebekah overheard these plans and made some plans of her own. She quickly maneuvered Jacob into position to receive the birthright. For she felt that Esau was not a fit candidate for this blessing. Esau was a hunter and a hairy man, and Jacob was a plain man more on the domesticated side. Some time, well before this, Esau sold the birthright to Jacob his younger brother, on a day when he returned home from hunting in the field and was weary and hungry after taking nothing in his hunt. Jacob had made a pot of stew and bargained with Esau for the birthright in return for the stew. While this private deal between the brothers may or may not have been known by both parents, the fact remains that Jacob bought it fair and square. In addition to this, he was better suited for the position of being the future family priest and overseer. It seems that Esau was more oriented to please his self interests rather than the overall family interests.

Rebekah instructed Jacob to prepare a lamb for his father, and take the skins of the lamb and put them on his hands and arms, and dress in Esau's clothes so as to have the feel and scent of Esau, hoping to fool his father so that he would bestow the blessing on him before Esau returned from the hunt. This took place, and Jacob received the blessing of the family birthright. Esau was furious, as one might expect, and made plans to take his brother's life. When Rebekah discovered the plot, she sent Jacob away to her homeland for a while, hoping that Esau's wrath would cool.

One might think that Rebekah was at fault in her plans of deception, but, when everything is laid on the table and all facts are looked at fair and square, one can see how her spiritual insight and motherly instinct was at work to further the will of God in the life of her chosen son.

In other places in the scriptures, we find that it was God's plan for Jacob to be the recipient of this position. In Romans 9:13 we are told: *"As it is written, Jacob have I loved, but Esau have I hated."* This reference by the Apostle Paul is to the Prophet Malachi in chapter 1, verses 2 and 3. Of course, the word "hated" here does not mean a gross hatred or dislike as we may think today, but rather it shows a preference being made to Jacob over Esau. Since God is God, does it not seem reasonable that He could choose what He wants without consultation with His human creation? From this point on, God often referred to Himself as being the God of

Abraham, and of Isaac, and of Jacob; not the God of Esau.

Although this riff existed between the two brothers, God kept His word and made nations of both son's descendants. Jacob had twelve sons, which became the heads of the twelve tribes of Israel, which would become Jacob's future name. Esau also had sons whose descendants became known as Edom, or the Edomites. Both sons' descendants multiplied over the centuries to fulfill the blessing that Rebekah would become the mother of thousands of millions.

# Rachel and Leah

## *The Mothers Who Built Israel*

*"And all the people that were in the gate, and the elders, said, We are witnesses. The LORD make the woman that is come into thine house like Rachel and like Leah, which two did build the house of Israel: and do thou worthily in Ephratah, and be famous in Bethlehem"* (Ruth 4:11).

Rachel and Leah were sisters; Leah being the elder and Rachel the younger. They were the daughters of Laban, the brother of Rebekah who was the wife of Isaac, the son of Abraham. Rebekah and Isaac had twin sons, Esau and Jacob. Esau was Isaac's favored son while Jacob was Rebekah's favorite.

The granting of the family birthright was traditionally bestowed on the firstborn son of the family upon reaching adulthood. The birthright was like a will in that it granted the one bearing it the rights and honor of being the head of the family clan after the father's death. Esau having been born first was due this honor. But his nature and disposition made him unsuited for this responsibility while Jacob exhibited excellent characteristics for such a position. By special maneuverings of his mother Rebekah, Jacob disguised himself as his older brother and deceived his nearly blind father into giving him the blessing. Needless to say, this stirred the wrath of Esau and Jacob had to flee for his life. His mother sent him away to her homeland of Padanaram to her father's house for his safety.

The tiring journey took several days, with nightfall finding Jacob sleeping under the stars. On one such night, while using a stone as his pillow, God appeared to him in a vision of a ladder reaching into heaven with angels going up and down on it. In this vision God confirmed His blessing on Jacob as He had done for his father Isaac and his grand-father, Abraham before him. God reassured him of His protection and guidance promising to be with him to bless and protect him. Jacob called the name of this place Bethel, which means the house of God.

When Jacob reached Padanaram he came to a well of water and waited there while the shepherds came to water their flocks. As the shepherds came to the well, Jacob uncovered it by rolling away the stone which sat over the well's opening. It was at this instant that Rachel came with her father's sheep. Jacob watered her sheep for her inquiring as to whose daughter she was and was much pleased to learn that she was the daughter of his mother's brother, Laban. He was invited to abide at her father's house. This pleased Jacob very much for Rachel was very fair and beautiful, and it was love at first sight in his heart.

After agreeing to work seven years for Laban in return for the hand of his daughter, Rachel, in marriage, Jacob settled down to a joyous labor of love. His love for

Rachel was so intense that the seven years seemed but a few days to him. The time finally came for the much-anticipated wedding. As the custom was in those days the bride was covered with a veil for the wedding ceremony. Jacob took his new bride into his tent for the wedding night and, when the morning had dawned, Jacob discovered that he had been tricked into marrying the older sister, Leah. He immediately protested to Laban. Laban replied that it was not the custom in his country to give the younger daughter in marriage before the firstborn and he suggested that Jacob labor another seven years for Rachel. Jacob, knowing the crafty nature of his father-in-law knew there would be no other way to get the woman he truly loved, so he agreed to work the additional seven years.

Jacob settled down as the husband of two women and begin building his own home and family. As fate would have it (actually it was by God's design) the bride that he loved so much could not bear children. On the other hand, Leah, the bride of deception began to bare children unto Jacob. She bore four sons unto him. When the first son was born . . . *she called his name Reuben: for she said, Surely the LORD hath looked upon my affliction; now therefore my husband will love me"* (Genesis 29:32). When the second son was born, she said, *"Because the LORD hath heard that I was hated, he hath therefore given me this son also: and she called his name Simeon"* (verse 33). At the birth of her third son, she said: *". . . this time will my husband be joined unto me, because I have born him three sons: therefore was his name called Levi* (Verse 34). When the fourth son was born, she said: *"Now will I praise the LORD: therefore she called his name Judah; and left bearing"* (Verse 35).

As we look upon this segment of the life of Leah, we can see the frustration and pain in her heart and soul. First, she was overlooked in favor of her younger and somewhat conceded baby sister. She was rejected by her husband, because all his love was ravished on Rachel. She felt no connection with her husband and consequentially less and less connection with her sister over this absence of affection. She had great hopes that Jacob would grow to love her and accept her as a companion along with her sister, Rachel. As the years wore on, she began to lose any hope that she could ever be loved by Jacob as a wife. As the birth of each child came, her agony increased and her hopes faded.

With the birth of her fourth son, she seemed to have somewhat of a change of heart. She realized that regardless of her disappointing circumstances she still had ONE that loved her; ONE that cared; and ONE that was looking on with the power to reward her for her faithfulness, even in her most bitter trials. The birth of that fourth son changed her outlook and brought a blessed hope that she secretly carried in her heart daily. The abiding knowledge that her husband's God, yes, and now even her own God, loved her and would see her through. With this son's birth she said; *"Now will I praise the LORD."* She discovered the key to contentment and peace, the key that made up for the contention and emptiness she had felt for so many years. The key that changed it all was praising the God of Heaven with all her heart. She seemed to be experiencing what a prophet of Israel would say by divine inspiration a few hundred years later: *"Thou wilt keep him in perfect peace, whose mind is stayed on thee: because he trusteth in thee"* (Isaiah 26:3).

Trials of life tend to draw us closer to God, because they help us see our inadequacies and help to foster a trust in God. Many centuries later, the Apostle Paul would say in the New Testament; *"Therefore I take pleasure in infirmities, in reproaches, in necessities, in persecutions, in distresses for Christ's sake: for when I am weak, then am I strong"* (2 Corinthians 12:10).

Leah, even though being rejected by her husband Jacob, was favored by God. She had no way of knowing in her lifetime that through the linage of her fourth son, Judah, the promised Redeemer, the Christ Child would be born. This blessing far exceeded the temporal blessing that would last only for a short earthly lifespan of having the love of her husband. The son of her praise which she bore in her sorrow would be one of the important building blocks in the nation of Israel that would bless the entire world for all of eternity.

Rachel's disappointment of not being able to bear children weighted more heavily upon her with the birth of each of Leah's children. In her envy and pain, she cried out to Jacob in great frustration, *"Give me children, or else I die"* (Genesis 30:1). Jacob was angry with her reminding her that it was not he, but God who had withheld the fruit of her womb. With this reality settling upon her, Rachel devised a plan that would in some small way make her feel that she could experience motherhood. She offered her handmaid, Bilhah to Jacob saying, *". . . she shall bear upon my knees, that I may also have children by her* (Genesis 30:3).

Rachel's maid, Bilhah, bore two sons unto Jacob: Dan and Naphtali. Rachel said, *"With great wrestlings have I wrestled with my sister, and I have prevailed"* (verse 8). She felt a consolation in this arrangement and was temporarily appeased.

When Leah saw what was done by Rachel and that she could no longer have any more children with which to attract the love of her husband, she followed Rachel's example and offered her maid, Zilpah, to Jacob. Zilpah bore two sons to Jacob also namely; Gad, and Asher.

When Rachel saw that Leah's maid also bore Jacob two sons, in her mind this canceled out the supposed victory she had gained over her sister. They were back to where they were before the arrangement between their maids and Jacob. The feud between the two sisters was revived, and Rachel felt the need to find another remedy for her misfortune of being childless. Leah's son, Reuben, had found some mandrakes in a field and brought them to his mother. Rachel saw these and demanded that Leah give them to her. Leah's reply was:*"Is it a small matter that thou hast taken my husband?*

*and wouldest thou take away my son's mandrakes also?* (Verse 15). Rachel promised Leah that Jacob would meet with her that night in return for the mandrakes.

What was so important about mandrakes that made Rachel feel that she had to have them and that Leah's son, Reuben wanted his mother to have them? Mandrake is a rare plant that grows in the Mediterranean region and was considered to have qualities to aid in conception, especially if a woman was barren and could not otherwise have children. They were sometimes referred to as "love apples." Since both sisters were barren at this time, they each desired the mandrakes hoping to be able to conceive children. There was an intense desire in the hearts of all Hebrew women to mother children—especially male children—hoping to be in the lineage of the coming Messiah, who was promised by God to Abraham, the original father of the Hebrew race. The Psalmist referenced this desire in the following words in Psalm 127, verses 3-5: *"Lo, children are an heritage of the LORD: and the fruit of the womb is his reward.* (4) *As arrows are in the hand of a mighty man; so are children of the youth.*

(5) *Happy is the man that hath his quiver full of them: they shall not be ashamed, but they shall speak with the enemies in the gate."* With this insight, we can see that the wife would be in greater favor with her husband if she could bear him many sons. It would bring great contentment and fulfillment in her life as well as in the life of her husband.

To continue this story, let us see how the scriptures explain what happened. This is found in Genesis, chapter 30, verses 16-21: *"And Jacob came out of the field in the evening, and Leah went out to meet him, and said, Thou must come in unto me; for surely I have hired thee with my son's mandrakes. And he lay with her that night.* (17) *And God hearkened unto Leah, and she conceived, and bare Jacob the fifth son.* (18) *And Leah said, God hath given me my hire, because I have given my maiden to my husband: and she called his name Issachar.* (19) *And Leah conceived again, and bare Jacob the sixth son.* (20) *And Leah said, God hath endued me with a good dowry; now will my husband dwell with me, because I have born him six sons: and she called his name Zebulun.* (21) *And afterwards she bare a daughter, and called her name Dinah."*

This welcome turn of events put Leah in the lead again in the race for motherhood and for the first place in the heart of her husband. Then God abruptly stepped into the picture and gave Rachel a leading role in this race with her sister. Genesis 30:22-24 tells it like this: *"And God remembered Rachel, and God hearkened to her, and opened her womb.* (23) *And she conceived, and bare a son; and said, God hath taken away my reproach:* (24) *And she called his name Joseph; and said, The LORD shall add to me another son."*

After the birth of Joseph, the Lord appeared unto Jacob and told him to return to his own country and to his kindred. He gathered his family and flocks together and prepared to leave Padanaram. His father-in-law pursued and overtook him with intentions of forcing him to turn back, for he did not want to see his daughters and grandchildren leave him. But God rebuked him in a dream the night before overtaking them and warned him not to do them any harm. Upon overtaking them he bid them farewell and kissed his children goodbye. Jacob journeyed on toward his homeland. When he got nearer his home, his brother Esau heard that he was coming and he prepared to come out to meet him. When Jacob heard this news, he was greatly troubled and sent his family across a brook for safety, and he prayed alone all night to God for divine protection. An angel of the Lord appeared to Jacob and wrestled with him all night. When the day was breaking, the angel intreated Jacob to let him go, but Jacob refused until the angel promised to bless him. The angel said unto him; *"Thy name shall be called no more Jacob, but Israel: for as a prince hast thou power with God and with men, and hast prevailed.* (30*) And Jacob called the name of the place Peniel: for I have seen God face to face, and my life is preserved"* (Genesis 32:28 and 30).

When Jacob met Esau, he was pleasantly relieved, for Esau was no longer angry with him. Their differences melted away to Jacob's great relief. As Jacob continued on toward his boyhood home, he stopped at Bethel, where God appeared to him in the vision many years before and there built an altar and worshipped God. As he left Bethel, he journeyed on toward Bethlehem. On the way there is where we see the last chapter of Rachel's life unfold. The scriptures tell it like this in Genesis 35:16-20.

*"And they journeyed from Bethel; and there was but a little way to come to Ephrath: and Rachel travailed, and she had hard labour.* (17) *And it came to pass, when she was in hard labour, that the midwife said unto her, Fear not; thou shalt have this son also.* (18) *And it came to pass, as her soul was in departing, (for she died) that she called his name Benoni: but his father called him Benjamin.* (19) *And Rachel died, and was buried in the way to Ephrath, which is Bethlehem.* (20) *And Jacob set a pillar upon her grave: that is the pillar of Rachel's grave unto this day."*

Let us end this narrative by looking at the legacy of each sister separately. We will look at Leah first, since she was the first wife. Leah's legacy was somewhat analogous to being more secular or everyday in nature.

Leah's relationship with Jacob was the product of deception and greed. Her father, Laban, deceived Jacob at the wedding by deceptively forcing Leah on Jacob. And then he tricked him into an additional seven years of servitude for his true love. The results were difficult and unfair to both her and Jacob. Jacob could never feel the love for her that he so fervently felt for her sister, Rachel. She could never realize true contentment under such conditions, and would always be envious of Rachel. Her life was bound up by these unfavorable conditions which trapped her in continuous pain and sorrow. She hoped even beyond hope with the birth of each of her children that this situation would change, but it never did. But there was a silver lining around her dark cloud, which she would come to recognize in later years.

After the death of Rachel, Jacob was left with only one wife, and it came down to his accepting and caring for Leah as his companion. There must have been some veneration, or at least a reserved acceptance of Leah, as Jacob would need some nurturing and comforting after losing his beloved Rachel. It was left to faithful Leah to rear Rachel's baby son for Jacob, a son that he would jealously protect and pamper. She faithfully performed these acts of love and devotion for her husband. The biblical record shows that she lived to an old age and had the honor of being buried in the family burial place, which was a cave purchased by Abraham in the field of Machpelah in the land of Canaan. There, Abraham and Sarah were buried along with Isaac and Rebekah. Jacob gave instructions to his sons to bury him there also, alongside his wife, Leah. She received little consolation in her life, but, in her death, she had the honor of resting in peace alongside her husband, while her sister was buried in a lonely desolate place along a road en route to Bethlehem.

The legacy of Rachel was determinedly spiritual in nature. There are many types and shadows in Scripture to bear this out. First of all, it was her firstborn son, Joseph, whom God used to preserve the life of the family of Jacob, which would later become the nation of

Israel—God's chosen nation from all the nations on Earth.

Briefly, Joseph was sold into Egypt by his brothers, who were jealous of him because of his dreams and the favor he had with their father. He was falsely accused, and found himself in Pharaoh's prison in Egypt. God used all these events to prepare Joseph for a marvelous work. When the set time came, God caused Pharaoh to dream two dreams that would trouble him greatly. Joseph was called by Pharaoh to interpret these dreams, which meant that a great seven-year famine was coming that would cover all the Earth. Pharaoh was so impressed with Joseph's recommendations on how to deal with the famine that he placed him over the land of Egypt to prepare for the preservation of life. The spiritual type here is that Joseph was a type of Christ, saving his family as Christ came to save the lost world.

Rachel was the wife of choice and the true love of Jacob. This position in Jacob's heart and life would make her the representative of God's purpose and grace to the nation that was to come from the family of Jacob. In type and shadow, she represented the mother of Israel as related in the events around the birth of Christ.

When the wise men from the east (astronomers most probably from Persia or Arabia) came to Jerusalem to worship the Christ Child after seeing His star, they were warned by God in a dream not to tell the wicked King

Herod where the child was. Consequently, they returned to their country another way.

When Herod found that he had been tricked by the wise men, he went and killed all the baby boys under the age of two years to prevent this "new born king" from growing up to be his rival. Scripture tells it like this: *"Then Herod, when he saw that he was mocked of the wise men, was exceeding wroth, and sent forth, and slew all the children that were in Bethlehem, and in all the coasts thereof, from two years old and under, according to the time which he had diligently enquired of the wise men.* (17) *Then was fulfilled that which was spoken by Jeremy the prophet, saying,*

(18) *In Rama was there a voice heard, lamentation, and weeping, and great mourning, Rachel weeping for her children, and would not be comforted, because they are not"* (Matthew 2:16-18).

Many dear mothers around the vicinity of Bethlehem were greatly grieved and hurt in seeing their precious babies being mercilessly killed. As Scripture says, there was *"lamentation, and weeping, and great mourning"* and they refused to be comforted over the loss of their irreplaceable children. The many mothers collectively were depicted in this scripture as being Jacob's beloved, Rachel. She was represented as the face of all the unnamed, hurting mothers of Bethlehem. This spiritual honor is quiet a legacy for a mother of long ago, who, against hope, waited on God and was rewarded with two sons with which to help build the nation of Israel. Rachel and Leah were truly the mothers (with their two maids) who built the nation of Israel with each of their sons forming a tribe of the nation.

# Jochebed

## *A Mother of Foresight*

*"And when she could not longer hide him, she took for him an ark of bulrushes, and daubed it with slime and with pitch, and put the child therein; and she laid it in the flags by the river's brink."* (Exodus 2:3)

The biblical narrative of the birth and childhood of Moses is very scant. Only a few verses, about a dozen in both the Old and New Testaments, reflect upon this aspect of Moses' life. Even the name of his mother is withheld in the initial biblical account of his birth. It was not until the recording of the family lineage of the tribes of Israel, near the time of their departure from Egypt, and the instructions by God to Moses to take a census of the children of Israel to determine their fighting capacity, and the dividing of the land for each tribe's inheritance that the mother of Moses is named. You can find these references in the books of Exodus and Numbers.

*"And Amram took him Jochebed his father's sister to wife; and she bare him Aaron and Moses: and the years of the life of Amram were an hundred and thirty and seven years"* (Exodus 6:20).

*"And the name of Amram's wife was Jochebed, the daughter of Levi, whom her mother bare to Levi in Egypt: and*

*she bare unto Amram Aaron and Moses, and Miriam their sister."* (Numbers 26:59)

The biblical narrative of the birth of Moses is short and to the point and is found in Exodus chapter 2, verses 1-10: *"And there went a man of the house of Levi, and took to wife a daughter of Levi.*

2 *And the woman conceived, and bare a son: and when she saw him that he was a goodly child, she hid him three months.*

3 *And when she could not longer hide him, she took for him an ark of bulrushes, and daubed it with slime and with pitch, and put the child therein; and she laid it in the flags by the river's brink.*

4 *And his sister stood afar off, to wit what would be done to him.*

5 *And the daughter of Pharaoh came down to wash herself at the river; and her maidens walked along by the river's side; and when she saw the ark among the flags, she sent her maid to fetch it.*

6 *And when she had opened it, she saw the child: and, behold, the babe wept. And she had compassion on him, and said, This is one of the Hebrews' children.*

7 *Then said his sister to Pharaoh's daughter, Shall I go and call to thee a nurse of the Hebrew women, that she may nurse the child for thee?*

8 *And Pharaoh's daughter said to her, Go. And the maid went and called the child's mother.*

9 *And Pharaoh's daughter said unto her, Take this child away, and nurse it for me, and I will give thee thy wages. And the woman took the child, and nursed it.*

10 *And the child grew, and she brought him unto Pharaoh's daughter, and he became her son. And she called his name Moses: and she said, Because I drew him out of the water."*

It was 430 years from the time that Jacob brought his family of 70 souls into Egypt (71, counting Joseph, who was already there) until they left Egypt under the mighty hand of God and the leadership of Moses. During this time, they multiplied greatly. Some estimates are believed to be in the millions. From the king of Egypt's vantage point, they became a crucial threat to the security of the country. He therefore issued an edict that the midwives should kill all the male babies that were born to the Israelite women. When the midwives refused, with the excuse that the Israelite women were stronger than the Egyptian women and had their babies before the midwives could get to them, the king ordered that all male babies be cast into the Nile River to be drowned immediately after birth. This is why the mother of Moses hid him for three months after his birth. When she could no longer hide him, she devised a method to save him by placing him into a basket and putting it into the river where she knew the daughter of Pharaoh, king of Egypt was apt to find him. She was praying and hoping that he would be rescued and his life spared.

The scriptural account states; "*and when she saw him that he was a goodly child, she hid him three months.*" Most Bible commentators suggest that the word *goodly* denotes being beautiful or very favorably in appearance. The New Testament reference in the book of Hebrews states it on this wise: *"By faith Moses, when he was born, was hid three months of his parents, because they saw he was a proper child; and they were not afraid of the king's commandment"* (Hebrews 11:23). Some biblical scholars attach a special divine influence from God upon his parents by the use of these two words; "goodly" and "proper" and by the phrase *"and they were not afraid of the king's commandment."* Be that as it may the plan worked and Moses was rescued from the water and became the adopted son of the daughter of Pharaoh. He was brought up in the courts of Egypt and raised in royalty and was in line to become a future Pharaoh of the land of Egypt.

When Moses became of age and was able to discern the differences between his adopted people and his birth people, he *"refused to be called the son of Pharaoh's daughter; Choosing rather to suffer affliction with the people of God, than to enjoy the pleasures of sin for a season"* (Hebrews 11:24, 25).

It seems reasonable that his choice may have rested with a maternal influence upon his young life by an unknown woman, who he perhaps never knew was his actual mother. This is where the greatness of his mother, Jochebed comes into play. Let's look at her godly virtues and how they shaped the destiny of a people who we know to be the downtrodden people of the Almighty God.

First, she was a descendent of Abraham who lived in a hostile foreign land. This was not to her credit, because she could not help who she was or where she lived. The thing that mattered is that she did not let her circumstances bring her defeat. Many who are trapped under unfavorable circumstances tend to become bitter and rebellious, which ends up making their lives worse instead of better.

Second, she was a woman of faith. The scriptures attest to this, and so do her actions and the godly influence she had on her son. Her faith enabled her to see something special in her third child, and she was determined to save him—even at the risk of her own life. First, she hid him as long as she could. When this was no longer feasible, she devised and put into action a plan that could save his life. She took a basket and made it watertight, and put it into the same river in which Pharaoh ordered all the baby boys to be drowned. By her faith, the instrument of death became the instrument of salvation for her young child. She instructed his sister, Miriam to stand guard and watch to see what would become of him.

The plan worked, for Pharaoh's daughter came to the river to bathe herself, and when she saw the basket floating among the reeds near the river's edge, she sent her maid to fetch it. When she opened it, she saw the beautiful child weeping, as his big eyes looked into hers. This melted her heart, and she purposed to take the child as her own and raise him as an Egyptian.

At this point, his sister came running to ask the daughter of Pharaoh if she could find a nurse for the child. Of course, the nurse she had in mind was his own mother. To this the Pharaoh's daughter consented and she sent the child back to his mother to be nurtured until he was old enough to be weaned.

It must be concluded that his mother wasted no time in training him in the ways of God and implanting into his tender child heart the knowledge of the true God of heaven. I am sure that she watered her teaching with tears in prayer for her son, as she knew that she had but a short time to get the most important work of her life completed. Once she turned him back over to Pharaoh's daughter, she would have no more opportunity to influence her precious child in the ways of God. How her godly heart must have ached when the time came to say goodbye to her most precious gift from God. I am most certain that she relinquished him into the care and authority of Egypt's ruling class with a prayer of faith and love in her heart that God would take the precious seed that she had planted into her young son's heart and nurture it and cause it to come to spiritual maturity at the proper future time, which God would ordain.

God rewarded her work of faith, as history records, and her son, Moses, (whom she did not even have the privilege of naming) became the most important figure in all of the Old Testament. For he was a direct type and shadow of Christ Himself who was to come to save all the world from its enemy, Satan, who is the prince and power of the air (Ephesians 2:2). One must stand in awe to see the hand of God working out the affairs of all humankind as His own divine will is unfolding before our very eyes.

To say that the mother of Moses was a mother of foresight is a befitting testimony to her character. For indeed she had great foresight, as her faith and actions proved. Whether she lived to see her son become a great leader, or whether she was still alive during the time of the exodus from Egypt, we do not know. But it seems that by faith she saw some divine purpose in God saving her son from the hand of the wicked Pharaoh, and she did not hesitate to act upon her faith. Millions of people have benefited spiritually from her simple faith and her fearless love for her infant son, upon whom, she evidently believed, the hand of God rested.

To our human minds it is sometimes strange how God works His wondrous will upon Earth. Many times, God takes the frail and weak among men and uses them to perform His awesome works. I personally know of cases where some persons who have done a great work for God were frail and almost perished as infants. Many who were disadvantaged as children, or who suffered setbacks in later life, overcame great obstacles to become well-known figures of society. Consider the following: Franklin D. Roosevelt led the United States through one of its toughest times during World War II from a wheelchair, being stricken with polio; Helen Keller, who was born blind and, in her early childhood, became deaf, was the first deaf and blind person to obtain a college degree and went on to learn several foreign languages and was an author of twelve published books. The world-famous composer, Beethoven, composed most of his famous works after becoming deaf. The scriptures speak of such phenomenal workings of God. Follow this thought with me in the following verses of Scripture.

*"Thy tacklings are loosed; they could not well strengthen their mast, they could not spread the sail: then is the prey of a great spoil divided;* ***the lame take the prey****"* (Isaiah 33:23).

*"But God hath chosen the foolish things of the world to confound the wise; and God hath chosen the weak things of the world to confound the things which are mighty;*

*28 And base things of the world, and things which are despised, hath God chosen, yea, and things which are not, to bring to nought things that are"* (1 Corinthians 1:27, 28).

Scripture gives the reason why God works in this manner: *"That no flesh should glory in his presence"* (verse 29).

Even thought Moses rose to become the most influential person in the Bible outside of the person of Christ, he was also very humble and meek as the following scripture tells us of him: *"Now the man Moses was very meek, above all the men which were upon the face of the earth"* (Numbers 12:3). Could it be that this bedrock of meekness was instilled in him in faith by his mother, Jochebed, as she taught him the fear of God in his youth? Her foresight seems to indicate that it very well might have been.

# Naomi

## *A Mother of Perseverance*

*"And she said unto them, Call me not Naomi, call me Mara: for the Almighty hath dealt very bitterly with me. I went out full, and the LORD hath brought me home again empty: why then call ye me Naomi, seeing the LORD hath testified against me, and the Almighty hath afflicted me?"* (Ruth 1:20, 21)

In the days of the Judges of Israel there was a man of Bethlehem whose name was Elimelech. His wife's name was Naomi and his two sons were Mahlon and Chilion. A famine developed in the land of Israel and Elimelech took his family and went into the land of Moab to live while the famine was upon the land of Israel.

The Moabitish people were descendants of Lot through his offspring by his eldest daughter. Before the destruction of Sodom and Gomorrah, Lot and his two daughters were brought forth out of the city of Sodom for their safety in direct answer to the prayer of his uncle, Abraham. Lot's wife left the city with them, but was turned into a pillar of salt because she looked back in disobedience of the Angels who came to rescue them.

Lot's sons-in-law refused to come with them out of the city, and were destroyed with the rest of the city because the sins of Sodom were in their hearts. Evidently the same was true of Lot's wife and that is why she had to take one last look at the city she loved and dreaded to leave. The daughters of Lot had no children because of the corruption of the lifestyle of their husbands. When they were out of the destroyed city and had settled down somewhat, they devised a plan to raise up offspring to their father since they had none by their erring husbands who were now destroyed. They enticed their father into a drunken stupor and each bore a son as a result. In their minds they were preserving the lineage of their father's name so it would not be forgotten after his death.

The land territory of Moab was bordered on the west by the Salt (Dead) Sea and on the east by the Arabian Desert. Israel was to the west of Moab on the other side of the Dead Sea. The same territory is now modern day Jordan.

Sometime after Elimelch reached Moab he died and his two sons took wives of the Mobitish women. The name of one was Orpah and the other's name was Ruth. Sometime later both the sons died also leaving the three women alone.

After their deaths, Naomi heard that the famine had lifted off the land in Israel and she determined to return to her homeland and to her people. She called her daughters-in-law unto her to bid them goodbye. They both objected to her leaving them, but, after some persuading, Orpah turned away to her own people. But Ruth clung unto her with these famous words: *"Intreat me not to leave thee, or to return from following after thee: for whither thou goest, I will go; and where thou lodgest, I will lodge: thy people shall be my people, and thy God my God: Where thou diest, will I die, and there will I be buried: the LORD do so to me, and more also, if ought but death part thee and me"* (Ruth 1:16, 17).

Upon returning to Bethlehem the people came out to greet her and welcome her back home. Her response was one of solemn reflection of her past and portrayed a trace of bitterness she felt in her heart over her losses. *"And she said unto them, Call me not Naomi, call me Mara: for the Almighty hath dealt very bitterly with me. I went out full, and the LORD hath brought me home again empty: why then call ye me Naomi, seeing the LORD hath testified against me, and the Almighty hath afflicted me?* (Ruth 1:20, 21).

It is true that Naomi experienced a tremendous loss. She lost her home in Israel; she lost her husband in death; she then lost her two sons in death. She was left with no one to look after her and care for her in her old age. She felt rejected, lost, and hopeless. She asked her friends to call her Mara, which means bitter because that is the way she was feeling. She was in the night time of her life.

The scriptures tell us that God gives a song in the night. A song is symbolic of hope and comfort. She was feeling everything but comfort in her seemingly hopeless condition. In her pain she could not hear the song in the night that God had sent her. She could not experience the comfort of her special song until some of the hurt had time to heal. This special song that God gave to her was her daughter-in-law, Ruth. The heart of Ruth was pure and true. She had pledged to stand by Naomi and accept her people as her own and her God as her own. God saw this quality in Ruth, and blessed both her and Naomi as a result.

One of her future offspring, through her faithful daughter-in-law, Ruth, three generations removed from her in time would say: *"For his anger endureth but a moment; in his favour is life: weeping may endure for a night, but joy cometh in the morning"* (Psalm 30:5). Morning would soon come to Naomi, and the first ray of daybreak was already with her, but she could not discern it. It was Ruth. The joy would be found in how God would use her in the near future to not only bless them in the present, but to be a blessing to all the world for generations to come. For ONE among Ruth's descendants would be Christ, the Saviour of the world.

Many people have experienced a time of setback with sorrow, grief, and loss at one time or another in their lives. It is in these times that some take their own lives. Others grow bitter and make life miserable, not only for themselves, but for others who are close and dear to them. But thanks to God there are some who count their losses and commit their lives to God and become instruments in God's hands to bless others through their own unpleasant experiences. It is these who God uses to comfort and inspire others as they experience hurt or loss for the first time and do not know how to deal with it. Christ was our example in dealing with hurt and disappointment. It is said of Him in Hebrews 2:18: *"For in that he himself hath suffered being tempted, he is able to succour them that are tempted."* The word "succor" means to help or give relief to those in need.

Naomi and Ruth returned to Bethlehem at the time of the barley harvest. As the custom was in those days, reapers, in the persons of young men, would cut the stalks of grain and bind them to haul to the threshing floor to beat out the grain for food. The gleaners were the maidens who would follow along behind them and pick up the pieces that fell to the ground. This method provided a means of survival for the very poor that were not able to work full time to provide for their own livelihood. Ruth became a gleaner of grain and by God's providence was led to glean in the field of Boaz, one of Naomi's well-to-do kinsman. He took a liking to her and instructed the young men to leave handfuls on purpose for her to glean. When Naomi found out this news, she instructed Ruth in the local customs, and Ruth willingly obeyed her mother-in-law, and the result was a marriage between the elderly man Boaz and the young Moabitish woman, Ruth.

The people of Bethlehem were very pleased with this marriage between Boaz and Ruth. Boaz was a well known and respected citizen and Ruth was the faithful daughter-in-law of another respected family from the area. Their hearts were moved with compassion and joy in seeing all the things that had befallen Naomi in the last several years and seeing her return with a faithful and beloved "daughter." They pronounced the following congratulatory blessing upon them. *"And all the people that were in the gate, and the elders, said, We are witnesses. The LORD make the woman that is come into thine house like Rachel and like Leah, which two did build the house of Israel: and do thou worthily in Ephratah, and be famous in Bethlehem: And let thy house be like the house of Pharez, whom Tamar bare unto Judah, of the seed which the LORD shall give thee of this young woman"* (Ruth 4:11, 12).

Their marriage produced a son, and the townswomen said unto Naomi; *"Blessed be the LORD, which hath not left thee this day without a kinsman, that his name may be famous in Israel. And he shall be unto thee a restorer of thy life, and a nourisher of thine old age: for thy daughter in law, which loveth thee, which is better to thee than seven sons, hath born him* (Ruth 4:14, 15).

The scriptural account in verses 16 and17 goes on to say: *"And Naomi took the child, and laid it in her bosom, and became nurse unto it. And the women her neighbours gave it a name, saying, There is a son born to Naomi; and they called his name Obed: he is the father of Jesse, the father of David."*

Naomi's life, not unlike many other people was typical of ups and downs with nothing apparently special about it to write home about. She may have experienced a bit more disappointments than many of us, but we all suffer some unpleasant things at one time or another. Her human nature shone through in her appraisal of her condition. We are all subject to feel badly about things that happen that are out of our control. But if we wait on the Lord, He will bring into our lives some purpose and meaning that we can weigh our disappointments against and see God's hand through it all. When we put our lives into true godly perspective our bitterness and disappointments will began to fade and we will begin to experience the joy that the Psalmist David spoke about. Naomi lived to see this time of joy in her senior years and it brought her the healing comfort that she had lacked for many years.

When we are faithful to God, He will fulfill His Word in our lives. We find this reassurance in Hebrews 13:5 *"Let your conversation be without covetousness; and be content with such things as ye have: for he hath said, I will never leave thee, nor forsake thee."*

We don't have to be a notable or famous person, or accomplish some great work in order for God to use us and make us a blessing to others. Naomi was just an ordinary woman and mother, but God saw fit to include a book in the Bible about her and her struggles. God is omniscient and He cares about each of us as if we were the only one in the whole world. My friend, do not be despondent about your place in the scheme of things or your seeming losses. If we will allow Him to, God will bless us and make us contented and happy with the place He has ordered for us in His great eternal plan for our lives.

# Hannah

## *A Mother of Prayer*

*"For this child I prayed; and the LORD hath given me my petition which I asked of him: Therefore also I have lent him to the LORD; as long as he liveth he shall be lent to the LORD. And he worshipped the LORD there"* (1 Samuel 1:27, 28).

In the days of the Judges of Israel there was a man of Ramah of mount Ephraim whose name was Elkanah. He had two wives, Hannah and Peninnah. Peninnah had children but Hannah was barren and could not bear children. Just how many children Peninnah had is not certain but Scripture says of her that she had sons and daughters.

It is believed by most Bible scholars and commentators that Elkanah married Hannah first and then married Peninnah later after finding that Hannah was barren. In those days it was considered a curse for a man not to have children to pass on his family name. Therefore, it seems reasonable that Hannah was his first wife and his first love, for his confession to her when seeing her grieved and troubled over her childless condition was *"why is thy heart grieved? am not I better to thee than ten sons?"* (1 Samuel 1:8). Some scholars suggest that perhaps Peninnah had ten sons besides her daughters and that was why Elkanah expressed his love to her in that manner.

Each year the family traveled to Shiloh to worship God as the custom was for all Jewish families in those days. Shiloh was the location of the Tabernacle which was the center of worship for the Jews at that time. Centuries later the center of worship would be at the Temple that King Solomon would build in Jerusalem.

Animal sacrifices were offered in worship during the week's festivals. The families would feast on the leftover portions of the sacrifices after due worship and dedication was offered to God. During these feast times Elkanah would give portions to Peninnah and her children and he would give a "worthy portion" to his wife, Hannah, because he loved her. The worthy portion was better and bigger than the regular portions received by the rest of the family. This "worthy portion" was a means of showing his love for her and to help to appease her over her not being able to have children of her own.

These feast times were especially burdensome to Hannah each year as they went to the appointed yearly worship. Elkanah's other wife Peninnah, would contemptuously provoke her incessantly throughout these feast times. Hannah's heart would ache as she wept sorely in silence over her sad state of affairs. Each year she dreaded the trip to Shiloh far she was made to relive this mockery and injustice that was arrogantly heaped upon her by the rival wife. If indeed Peninnah did have ten sons and some daughters as speculated, the time element would have been several years, at least twelve and perhaps even twenty or more that Hannah would have had to endure this emotional abuse.

After many years of suffering, she came to the point when she realized that enough was enough. Unlike Rachel, when she could not have children, Hannah did not blame her husband, but rather purposed in her heart to petition God for an answer by giving her a special miracle. It was during one of these feasts at Shiloh that she stole away from the family and went into the Tabernacle to pray to God for a son of her own. The many years of disappointment had conditioned her to have faith in God, seeing that He was the only one that could change the situation. Her maternal instinct fostered a strong desire for children of her own. But as time wore on the spiritual nature of her faithful heart wanted a son, not only for herself, but one that she could dedicate to God as a permanent servant who would become a spiritual leader of the house of Israel.

At this point in time, the nation of Israel had fallen into gross neglect and spiritual darkness. Scripture described it as being a time when there was *"no open vision"* meaning that God had ceased to speak to them as a nation because they had turned their back upon Him as they had done so many times before. They were merely going through the motions of worship without their heart being in what they were doing. Eli was the priest of God at this time, but did not perform his duties faithfully. He refused to restrain his evil sons who were taking advantage of the people when they came to worship.

In times like these when the people needed direction there was no one to lead them in true worship. The nation was falling apart and no one seemed able to lead them back to a proper relationship with God. During such times, God searches for one who He can ordain for a special work. Usually, God's man will be one who has gone through hard trials and had many set-backs and disappointments. For it is this type of person who will engage his heart to seek God to hear His voice and receive direction from Him. It is also this type of person that God knows He can depend on.

God needed such a one to turn His called-out nation of Israel back to Him. He would find such a one as He always does, but first there must be a detour. This temporary detour would be accomplished through a woman—a woman who had great faith, whose faith was the result of great suffering which drove her to fervent prayer. Her suffering was designed by God for His divine purpose of using her in the raising up of a prophet and priest in Israel through a son that would be born to her in answer to her earnest praying, the kind of praying that would produce a miracle, a miracle of conceiving a son in her old age for the future purpose and glory of God.

We will let the scriptures tell the story, for they can tell it better than I. These scriptures are First Samuel 1: 9-18:

*"So Hannah rose up after they had eaten in Shiloh, and after they had drunk. Now Eli the priest sat upon a seat by a post of the temple of the LORD.* (10) *And she was in bitterness of soul, and prayed unto the LORD, and wept sore.* (11) *And she vowed a vow, and said, O LORD of hosts, if thou wilt indeed look on the affliction of thine handmaid, and remember me, and not forget thine handmaid, but wilt give unto thine handmaid a man child, then I will give him unto the LORD all the days of his life, and there shall no razor come upon his head.* (12) *And it came to pass, as she continued praying before the LORD, that Eli marked her mouth.*

(13) *Now Hannah, she spake in her heart; only her lips moved, but her voice was not heard: therefore Eli thought she had been drunken.* (14) *And Eli said unto her, How long wilt thou be drunken? put away thy wine from thee.* (15) *And Hannah answered and said, No, my lord, I am a woman of a sorrowful spirit: I have drunk neither wine nor strong drink, but have poured out my soul before the LORD.* (16) *Count not thine handmaid for a daughter of Belial: for out of the abundance of my complaint and grief have I spoken hitherto.* (17) *Then Eli answered and said, Go in peace: and the God of Israel grant thee thy petition that thou hast asked of him.* (18) *And she said, Let thine handmaid find grace in thy sight. So the woman went her way, and did eat, and her countenance was no more sad.*

The family returned home from the feast and during the course of the following year Hannah conceived and bore a son and called his name Samuel, which means being asked of the Lord. Hannah refused to go to Shiloh for the next few years in order to stay home and take care of her son until he could be weaned. Being weaned meant much more during those times than it does in today's society. We usually think of a child being weaned when he is able to leave the bottle or breast and graduate to solid food. Also being toilet trained plays into the formula as well. The third aspect of being weaned in those days was an initial teaching process to establish a foundation for the future life of the child. This element is sadly missing in most of today's childrearing syllabuses. Moses's mother, Jochebed and Hannah, the mother of Samuel were shining examples in this aspect of child weaning in Bible times.

As Hannah stayed behind, she cared for her son until he was old enough to function independently. She taught him the ways of the Lord and instilled in his tender heart the love and fear of God. She, like the mother of Moses, had but a short time to mold and shape her precious son's character before relinquishing him to the care of another. After these precious short years of nurturing and training him she would have no more motherly influence in his life. This no doubt, would cause much pain to most mothers, but she had a higher goal with her son—one that would override the pain of temporary loss, knowing the value he would be to her nation and her God in the years ahead.

After Samuel was properly weaned, she brought him to Shiloh with an appropriate offering to God, to present him to Eli, the priest. *"And she said, Oh my lord, as thy soul liveth, my lord, I am the woman that stood by thee here, praying unto the LORD.* (27) *For this child I prayed; and the LORD hath given me my petition which I asked of him:* (28) *Therefore also I have lent him to the LORD; as long as he liveth he shall be lent to the LORD"* (1 Samuel 1:26-28).

Each year, Hannah would bring a little coat that the had lovingly made for Samuel when she returned for the annual feasts. I supposed Samuel must have looked forward to seeing his mother each year and receiving her gifts. Scripture says of him that *"the child did minister unto the LORD before Eli the priest."* Scripture goes on to bear out that Samuel grew in favor with both God and men and that all Israel knew that he was established to be a prophet of the LORD.

When Hannah brought him to present him to the Lord, she prayed a wonderful prophetic prayer as her heart overflowed with praise and adoration unto the Lord. That prayer is presented here as the Bible records it: *"My heart rejoiceth in the LORD, mine horn is exalted in the LORD: my mouth is enlarged over mine enemies; because I rejoice in thy salvation. There is none holy as the LORD: for there is none beside thee: neither is there any rock like our God. Talk no more so exceeding proudly; let not arrogancy come out of your mouth: for the LORD is a God of knowledge, and by him actions are weighed. The bows of the mighty men are broken, and they that stumbled are girded with strength. They that were full have hired out themselves for bread; and they that were hungry ceased: so that the barren hath born seven; and she that hath many children is waxed feeble. The LORD killeth, and maketh alive: he bringeth down to the grave, and bringeth up. The LORD maketh poor, and maketh rich: he bringeth low, and lifteth up. He raiseth up the poor out of the dust, and lifteth up the beggar from the dunghill, to set them among princes, and to make them inherit the throne of glory: for the pillars of the earth are the LORD'S, and he hath set the world upon them. He will keep the feet of his saints, and the wicked shall be silent in darkness; for by strength shall no man prevail. The adversaries of the LORD shall be broken to pieces; out of heaven shall he thunder upon them: the LORD shall judge the ends of the earth; and he shall give strength unto his king, and exalt the horn of his anointed"* (1 Samuel 2:1-10).

Hannah was truly a woman and a mother of prayer. Her first recorded prayer was one of exasperation and hope, and God answered her humble request by giving her the son of her heart's desire. Her last recorded prayer was one of triumph and joy as she poured out her heart in thanksgiving and praise to God. In today's terminology the great old hymn, *"How Great Thou Art,"* would most accurately describe what Hannah was feeling when she prayed this wonderful prayer.

God is so great, indeed. He not only gave Hannah a son as she asked of Him, but He went on to give her three other sons and two daughters. She asked for one son that she could give back to God. Instead, God gave her not only this son, but five other children that she could keep for her own! You just cannot out-give God. What a wonderful God is the God that we serve!

# Mary

## *The Mother of Jesus*

*"And the angel came in unto her, and said, Hail, thou that art highly favoured, the Lord is with thee: blessed art thou among women."* (Luke: 2:28)

Of all the mothers in all the world; past, present, and future, Mary was the most unique mother of all. Not only was she the most unique, but she was the most famous as well. Her fame stemmed not because she was from a well-to-do family, for she was not. Nor was she from a family that was famous. It is very probable that her family was not well known outside their home town area. Her folks were not noted for any great accomplishments or political achievements. She was just another ordinary young girl from an ordinary family background. There was no apparent difference between her and her peers. She did not choose her role in God's scheme of things any more than any one of us has done. Many other young ladies could have accomplished what she accomplished. Why then did Mary fulfill the most important role in the entire history of the human race? What set her apart and made her so special? Why was she the one to bring forth the Son of God into the human race? The answer is threefold. She was chosen of God. She found favor in God's sight. She was willing to obey God's directive by humbling herself and submitting to His divine will.

God's pre-determined will in choosing a mother for His Son and the favor He must find in the one chosen would involve the following four things: (1) She must be from the proper linage in Israel; (2) She must be a virgin; (3) Her family linage must have their roots in the town of Bethlehem where the Son of God was decreed by prophecy to be born; (4) She must live in the right time period for God to accomplished His perfect timing.

**Mary Was from the Right Tribe of Israel**

The earthly mother of God's Son by necessity would need to descend from the proper tribe of Israel. This tribe was the tribe of Judah according to Genesis 49:10. *"The sceptre shall not depart from Judah, nor a lawgiver from between his feet, until Shiloh come; and unto him shall the gathering of the people be."* The word, "Shiloh" in this scripture is a prophetic reference to Christ. This verse of Scripture indicates that Christ would come through the tribe of Judah. The earthly linage of Christ is traced back to Judah in the Gospels of Matthew and Luke. Matthew traces the linage through Joseph and Luke traces the linage through Mary.

**Mary Was a Virgin**

The long-awaited promised Messiah must be born of a virgin according to Isaiah 7:14. *"Therefore the Lord himself shall give you a sign; Behold, a virgin shall conceive, and bear a son, and shall call his name Immanuel."* Both, Matthew and Luke reveal the fact that Mary fit this prophetic requirement calling her a virgin. Matthew says: *"Now the birth of Jesus Christ was on this wise: When as his mother Mary was espoused to Joseph, before they came together, she was found with child of the Holy Ghost"* (Matthew 1:18). *"Now all this was done, that it might be fulfilled which was spoken of the Lord by the prophet, saying, Behold, a virgin shall be with child, and shall bring forth a son, and they shall call his name Emmanuel, which being interpreted is, God with us"* (Verses 22 and 23). Mathew adds even more weight to this fact in verse twenty-five of chapter one where he was speaking of Joseph when he said: *"And knew her not till she had brought forth her firstborn son: and he called his name JESUS."* The terminology, *"and knew her not"* indicates that they had no marital relations until after the baby was born. Not only did Matthew inform us that Mary was a virgin when Christ was conceived in her womb, but she remained a virgin until after Jesus was born.

Luke also made a special effort to let us know that Mary was a virgin when Christ was conceived. He said in Luke 1 and verse 27 that an angel was sent from God *"To a virgin espoused to a man whose name was Joseph, of the house of David; and the virgin's name was Mary."* In verses 34 and 35 Luke tells us of Mary's response to the angel and the counter response of the angel back to her. *"Then said Mary unto the angel, How shall this be, seeing I know not a man?* (35) *And the angel answered and said unto her, The Holy Ghost shall come upon thee, and the power of the Highest shall overshadow thee: therefore also that holy thing which shall be born of thee shall be called the Son of God."* Jesus was virgin born for without this miraculous birth He could not have been the Son of God.

**Christ Must Be Born in the Town of Bethlehem**

Jesus must be born in the town of Bethlehem as specified by the prophet Micah in his book in chapter five and verse two: *"But thou, Bethlehem Ephratah, though thou be little among the thousands of Judah, yet out of thee shall he come forth unto me that is to be ruler in Israel; whose goings forth have been from of old, from everlasting."* We can find this fulfillment in both Matthew and Luke. Mathew tells us in chapter 2, verses 1-6: *"Now when Jesus was born in Bethlehem of Judaea in the days of Herod the king, behold, there came wise men from the east to Jerusalem,* (2) *Saying, Where is he that is born King of the Jews? for we have seen his star in the east, and are come to worship him.* (3) *When Herod the king had heard these things, he was troubled, and all Jerusalem with him.* (4) *And when he had gathered all the chief priests and scribes of the people together, he demanded of them where Christ should be born. (5) And they said unto him, In Bethlehem of Judaea: for thus it is written by the prophet,*

(6) *And thou Bethlehem, in the land of Juda, art not the least among the princes of Juda: for out of thee shall come a Governor, that shall rule my people Israel."*

God set up the circumstances that made this prophecy possible by using a wicked king (Caesar Augustus) to bring about the fulfillment of His prophetic Word. Luke 2:1-7 nails this down for us. *"And it came to pass in those days, that there went out a decree from Caesar Augustus, that all the world should be taxed.* (2) *(And this taxing was first made when Cyrenius was governor of*

*Syria.)* (3) *And all went to be taxed, every one into his own city.* (4) *And Joseph also went up from Galilee, out of the city of Nazareth, into Judaea, unto the city of David, which is called Bethlehem; (because he was of the house and lineage of David:)* (5) *To be taxed with Mary his espoused wife, being great with child.* (6) *And so it was, that, while they were there, the days were accomplished that she should be delivered.* (7) *And she brought forth her firstborn son, and wrapped him in swaddling clothes, and laid him in a manger; because there was no room for them in the inn."*

**God's Timing Was Precise**

Scripture tells us in Galatians 4:4: *"But when the fulness of the time was come, God sent forth his Son, made of a woman, made under the law."* The *"fulness of time"* would occur at a point in time when the Old Testament Law period had fully run its course and the dawn of the day of Grace would come. The Children of Israel lived under the Law (which God gave through Moses) with the prophets being God's chief spokespersons. The Grace dispensation would get their teachings and directions through the Apostles which Christ would set up in His Church when He came on the scene. The scriptures explain it like this: *"For the law was given by Moses, but grace and truth came by Jesus Christ"* (John 1:17). The voice of Jesus is on record in Luke 16:16 where He expresses it this way: *"The law and the prophets were until John: since that time the kingdom of God is preached, and every man presseth into it."*

Jesus' statement above about the law and prophets being until John was a reference to John the Baptist.

There was a space of time of complete silence from Heaven for around four hundred years between the Old and New Testament time period. John the Baptist would come breaking this silence being the prophetic figure of the *"voice of one crying in the wilderness."* Luke, chapter 3, verses 3 and 4 tells us about this. *"And he came into all the country about Jordan, preaching the baptism of repentance for the remission of sins; As it is written in the book of the words of Esaias the prophet, saying, The voice of one crying in the wilderness, Prepare ye the way of the Lord, make his paths straight."* Jesus' testimony of John was: *"For I say unto you, Among those that are born of women there is not a greater prophet than John the Baptist: but he that is least in the kingdom of God is greater than he"* (Luke 7:28).

John was born to an elderly couple whose names were Elizabeth and Zacharias. Elizabeth was barren, but, like so many barren women in Bible times, God was saving her for a special birth. When she was six months with child, the angel of the Lord appeared to Mary to tell her of her role in the coming of the world's Saviour. The angel also informed Mary of Elizabeth being with child and Mary went and visited her for three months before the birth of John for Elizabeth and Mary were cousins. There was a spiritual and a natural connection between both mothers and both Sons. John's prophetic role of ministry was to blaze the way for the coming of Christ's ministry. He went before Him preaching repentance and baptizing the people. Their ministry complimented each other's; therefore, the synchronizing of the time-frame of their births was necessary.

Mary's role was determined before the foundation of the world. Jesus is called the Lamb of God in John 1:29. In Revelation 13:8 it is said of Christ that He was the Lamb (of God) slain from the foundation of the world. This prophecy was first given in Genesis 3:5: *"And I will put enmity between thee and the woman, and between thy seed and her seed; it shall bruise thy head, and thou shalt bruise his heel."* In this prophecy God was speaking to Satan who was represented in the form of the serpent which appeared to Eve to tempt her to take of the forbidden fruit and fall from grace into sin. The seed of the woman was a reference to Christ who would come to defeat Satan by His death on the cross and His glorious resurrection, victorious over death, hell, and the grave. With this act, Satan was eternally defeated once and for all time and our eternal redemption was secured.

This mystery of God is put into better focus in the apostle Paul's writing in Ephesians 3:9 *"And to make all men see what is the fellowship of the mystery, which from the beginning of the world hath been hid in God, who created all things by Jesus Christ."* All of God's works were determined by God long before he laid the foundation of the world. These divine mysteries were *"hid in God"* and are revealed as prophecies in the Word of God. These scriptures speak of the plan of God existing before the world was established and are made known to His creation (us) at the appointed time as we study His Word. So, if Christ was pre-ordained to be born into the human race to save us from our sins, then it stands to reason that the mother of Christ would have by necessity been pre-ordained as well. Mary was indeed born for this purpose. God raised her up to fulfill His will in bringing His only begotten Son into the world.

We usually think of this event as the "Christmas Story." The birth of Christ, which we celebrate as Christmas, is a special time of the year. I don't know of anyone who does not love and appreciate Christmas, unless it would be the fictitious character, Scrooge. While Christmas helps us remember the birth of Jesus, Christmas celebrations are not what it is all about. It is much more serious than this. The scriptures gives the real purpose of Christmas in Hebrews 9:24-28. *"For Christ is not entered into the holy places made with hands, which are the figures of the true; but into heaven itself, now to appear in the presence of God for us:* (25) *Nor yet that he should offer himself often, as the high priest entereth into the holy place every year with blood of others;* (26) *For then must he often have suffered since the foundation of the world: but now once in the end of the world hath he appeared to put away sin by the sacrifice of himself.* (27) *And as it is appointed unto men once to die, but after this the judgment:* (28) *So Christ was once offered to bear the sins of many; and unto them that look for him shall he appear the second time without sin unto salvation.*

This beautiful "Christmas" story has some bittersweet properties entwined within it. The birth of Christ was beautiful. For the most part, the life of Christ was beautiful as well. The end of His earthly human life was adversely bitter. But the eternal purpose and fulfillment is beautiful and glorious indeed.

We will now turn our attention more fully to Mary, the mother of the Christ Child, whose character seems to come through in a somewhat unassuming manner. It is presumed by many that Mary was a young girl, perhaps in her mid-teens when she was called upon to bear Christ into the world. It would be shocking and distressing to receive such an announcement as the one with which the angel appeared to Mary. Try to picture, if you can, the scene before us as the angel of the Lord suddenly appeared to a young woman, who no doubt was the last person in the world to anticipate such a grave event happening to her as that which the angel described so unexpectedly.

*"And in the sixth month* [of Elizabeth's pregnancy with John the Baptist] *the angel Gabriel was sent from God unto a city of Galilee, named Nazareth, To a virgin espoused to a man whose name was Joseph, of the house of David; and the virgin's name was Mary. And the angel came in unto her, and said, Hail, thou that art highly favoured, the Lord is with thee: blessed art thou among women. And when she saw him, she was troubled at his saying, and cast in her mind what manner of salutation this should be. And the angel said unto her, Fear not, Mary: for thou hast found favour with God. And, behold, thou shalt conceive in thy womb, and bring forth a son, and shalt call his name JESUS. He shall be great, and shall be called the Son of the Highest: and the Lord God shall*

*give unto him the throne of his father David: And he shall reign over the house of Jacob for ever; and of his kingdom there shall be no end."*

Her reaction was one of stunned disbelief and amazement. Her initial response to the angel was: ". . . *How shall this be, seeing I know not a man?* (Luke 1:34). The angel quickly informed her saying; *"The Holy Ghost shall come upon thee, and the power of the Highest shall overshadow thee: therefore also that holy thing which shall be born of thee shall be called the Son of God.* (36) *And, behold, thy cousin Elisabeth, she hath also conceived a son in her old age: and this is the sixth month with her, who was called barren. For with God nothing shall be impossible"* (Luke 1:35, 37). Somehow and in some manner unbeknown to us the power of God descended upon Mary and melted away all her fears. She responded joyfully and humbly: *"Behold the handmaid of the Lord; be it unto me according to thy word."* With this response the angel of the Lord disappeared as quickly as he appeared in the beginning.

Mary went immediately to visit Elizabeth and spent three months with her. When Mary arrived at the home of Elizabeth and gave her the news of what had happened with her, Elizabeth's baby leaped in her womb. Perhaps this was a confirmation of the connection of the ministries of both babies yet to be born. Mary returned back to Nazareth shortly before Caesar's decree for all people to go to their native city to be taxed. This taxing was more of a census but involved a tax for the Roman Emperor was greedy.

Mary and Joseph were from the town of Nazareth, a distance of about ninety miles from Bethlehem where Christ would be born. Can you just picture the grueling journey this must have been for Mary being great with child (in her late term of pregnancy) having to ride on the back of a donkey for this great distance? The mighty Caesar deemed it necessary for all his subjects to return to the place of their nativity to be counted in his census. In his mind he was doing what he thought proper but God moved him to require this in order that prophecy be fulfilled. God used an earthly king to get Mary to the town of Bethlehem for the birth of His Son. While we look back upon this today and understand its significance, it is most likely and very probable that Caesar Augusta never had an inkling of what was transpiring.

When the proper time came and the proper location was reached, Christ was born. His birth announcement was not a glittering embossed card, nor, as we might do today, a Facebook post that would go viral, but rather was a divine visitation of an angel from Heaven to a group of lowly shepherds on a hillside outside the town of Bethlehem with a glorious message of hope saying *"Fear not: for, behold, I bring you good tidings of great joy, which shall be to all people. For unto you is born this day in the city of David a Saviour, which is Christ the Lord. And this shall be a sign unto you; Ye shall find the babe wrapped in swaddling clothes, lying in a manger."* The angel was joined by a multitude of heavenly angels praising God and saying, *"Glory to God in the highest, and on earth peace, good will toward men"* (Luke 2:10-14).

Christ was born in a stable (a shelter for cattle) and laid in a manger (a feed trough) *"because there was no room for them in the inn"* (Luke 2:7). The shepherds came and found the newborn babe just as the angel had said. They blazed the news abroad before returning to their flocks.

When eight days were passed, the ceremonial circumcision was performed and He was officially given the name JESUS which God decreed by the angel before He was conceived. The Jewish Law demanded that the mother of a son go through a forty-day purification process and then take the child to the Temple to present Him to the Lord. As Mary and Joseph were in the process of doing this an elderly man and woman approached them and spoke prophetically about Him. We will digress to the scriptures for the unfolding of the story at this point for they tell it much better than I can.

*"And when eight days were accomplished for the circumcising of the child, his name was called JESUS, which was so named of the angel before he was conceived in the womb.* (22) *And when the days of her purification according to the law of Moses were accomplished, they brought him to Jerusalem, to present him to the Lord;* (23) *(As it is written in the law of the Lord, Every male that openeth the womb shall be called holy to the Lord;)* (24) *And to offer a sacrifice according to that which is said in the law of the Lord, A pair of*

*turtledoves, or two young pigeons.* (25) *And, behold, there was a man in Jerusalem, whose name was Simeon; and the same man was just and devout, waiting for the consolation of Israel: and the Holy Ghost was upon him.* (26) *And it was revealed unto him by the Holy Ghost, that he should not see death, before he had seen the Lord's Christ.* (27) *And he came by the Spirit into the temple: and when the parents brought in the child Jesus, to do for him after the custom of the law,* (28) *Then took he him up in his arms, and blessed God, and said,* (29) *Lord, now lettest thou thy servant depart in peace, according to thy word:* (30) *For mine eyes have seen thy salvation,* (31) *Which thou hast prepared before the face of all people;* (32) *A light to lighten the Gentiles, and the glory of thy people Israel.* (33) *And Joseph and his mother marvelled at those things which were spoken of him.* (34) *And Simeon blessed them, and said unto Mary his mother, Behold, this child is set for the fall and rising again of many in Israel; and for a sign which shall be spoken against;* (35) *(Yea, a sword shall pierce through thy own soul also,) that the thoughts of many hearts may be revealed.* (36) *And there was one Anna, a prophetess, the daughter of Phanuel, of the tribe of Aser: she was of a great age, and had lived with an husband seven years from her virginity;* (37) *And she was a widow of about fourscore and four years, which departed not from the temple, but served God with fastings and prayers night and day.* (38) *And she coming in that instant gave thanks likewise unto the Lord, and spake of him to all them that looked for redemption in Jerusalem.* (39) *And when they had performed all things according to the law of the Lord, they returned into Galilee, to their own city Nazareth.* (40) *And the child grew, and waxed strong in spirit, filled with wisdom: and the grace of God was upon him"* (Luke 2:21-40).

Only one incident in the boyhood years of Jesus is recorded in the scriptures. This involved the trip to Jerusalem when He was twelve years of age. He was left behind when they started on their way back to their home in Nazareth. After a day's journey they missed Him and returned to Jerusalem to search for Him. After three days of searching, they found Him in the Temple sitting in the midst of the doctors (of the Law, perhaps, meaning the Pharisees and possibly other Rabbi) listening to them and asking them questions. All were amazed at His profound wisdom, being only a Child. Mary scolded Him and His reply was *"How is it that ye sought me? Wist ye not that I must be about my Father's business?"* He returned home with them and was subject unto them and grew in favor with God and man. As a young man He took up the trade of carpentry as His stand-in or proxy father, Joseph, was a carpenter.

As was the case when the shepherds visited Him in the manger, Mary pondered all these things in her heart. Perhaps she pondered over many things throughout the coming years as He grew to manhood and began His ministry. Of all people she definitely knew that He was Divine and had a mission to fulfill which was ordained by His Father in Heaven.

As the years rolled on Mary and Joseph had other children. There were at least four more brothers and two or more sisters according to Matthew 13:53-57. *"And it came to pass, that when Jesus had finished these parables, he departed thence.* (54) *And when he was come into his own country, he taught them in their synagogue, insomuch that they were astonished, and said, Whence hath this man this wisdom, and these mighty works?* (55) *Is not this the carpenter's son? is not his mother called Mary? and his brethren, James, and Joses, and Simon, and Judas?* (56) *And his sisters, are they not all with us? Whence then hath this man all these things?* (57) *And they were offended in him. But Jesus said unto them, A prophet is not without honour, save in his own country, and in his own house."*

His own brothers did not believe in Him until about the time of His crucifixion and resurrection. The folks around where Jesus grew up had trouble accepting Him as the Messiah as did His own flesh and blood siblings. That is why Jesus made the statement in verse 57 above. But it is well to note, as revealed in the book of Acts, that His brother James, became the leader in chief of the Church after Christ ascended back into Heaven.

Mary and His siblings interacted with Him during His ministry. Mary was present at His very first miracle where He turned the water into wine during a wedding feast. She encouraged His disciples to obey whatever He was to say unto them. In Mark 3:31, 32 we see them seeking His attention probably over some domestic issue. *"There came then his brethren and his mother, and, standing without, sent unto him, calling him.* (32) *And the multitude sat about him, and they said unto him, Behold, thy mother and thy brethren without seek for thee."*

During the time of His crucifixion Mary was present at the cross giving her love and support unto Him. John 19:26 and 27 relates the following about this scene. *"When Jesus therefore saw his mother, and the disciple standing by, whom he loved, he saith unto his mother, Woman, behold thy son!* (27) *Then saith he to the disciple, Behold thy mother! And from that hour that disciple took her unto his own home."* John was the disciple spoken of here. He did not name himself in his writings, but simply referred to himself as *"the disciple whom Jesus loved."* Every leader has an inner circle of confidants and John was one of these.

It is believed by most historians that Joseph had died sometime during the formative years of Christ. No mention is made of him in the ministry years of Christ other than relating the fact that Jesus (in the eyes and understanding of society) was the son of Joseph, the carpenter. It seems that this is the reason Jesus directed His mother to take up her dwelling at the home of His beloved disciple, John, and why he instructed John to receive her as his own mother. Back in those days there were no social or governmental sponsored agencies in place to take care of the unfortunate. Jesus was looking after her needs beyond the time that He would spend on the earth. He knew that He could depend on His beloved disciple to take care of her in His absence.

Here, at this scene of the cross was fulfilled the saying of Simeon, the elderly man who patiently waited for the consolation of Israel (and yea, of the whole world, itself) when he proclaimed to Mary that the time would come when a sword would pierce through her soul. Only Mary, herself, knew the agony and grief she felt that day seeing her innocent miraculous born Divine Son of God suffering for the sins of all mankind, of all ages, and of all the whole world.

There is one more scene in the life of Mary that is noted in the scriptures and this is from the first chapter of the book of Acts. The disciples returned to Jerusalem after witnessing the Ascension of Jesus into heaven. Having been previously directed by the Lord, they congregated with other believers and waited for the promised coming of *"The Comforter"* (which is the Holy Ghost). This direction was given before Christ was crucified in Luke 24:49: *"And, behold, I send the promise of my Father upon you: but tarry ye in the city of Jerusalem, until ye be endued* [endowed or empowered] *with power from on high."* Acts 1:12-14 states: *"Then returned they unto Jerusalem from the mount called Olivet, which is from Jerusalem a sabbath day's journey.* (13) *And when they were come in, they went up into an upper room, where abode both Peter, and James, and John, and Andrew, Philip, and Thomas, Bartholomew, and Matthew, James the son of Alphaeus, and Simon Zelotes, and Judas the brother of James.* (14) *These all continued with one accord in prayer and supplication, with the women, and Mary the mother of Jesus, and with his brethren."*

This happened on the day of Pentecost, about forty days after His Ascension as recorded by Luke in Acts 2:1-4. *"And when the day of Pentecost was fully come, they were all with one accord in one place.* (2) *And suddenly there came a sound from heaven as of a rushing mighty wind, and it filled all the house where they were sitting.* (3) *And there appeared unto them cloven tongues like as of fire, and it sat upon each of them.* (40 *And they were all filled with the Holy Ghost, and began to speak with other tongues, as the Spirit gave them utterance."* Mary, the Mother of Jesus was present as a part of this group which consisted of about one hundred and twenty according to Acts 1:15.

Thus, ends the story of Mary, the Mother of Jesus, the Christ Child—chosen of God; faithful and true; and one who was highly favored by God, our Divine Creator. What an awesome life! What an awesome personality! Could anyone, anywhere, or at any time ever supersede such a role in life or high honor as God bestowed upon the relatively unknown, poor, but humble Jewish girl known simply as Mary, the earthly mother of His only begotten Son?!!!

## A Word about Reviews

As you are probably aware, reviews are the life blood of any author. They are what readers look at when selecting a book to purchase. I hope you've enjoyed *Biblical Mothers of Distinction*, and, if you have, won't you please take a moment to write a positive, descriptive review? Please cite what it was that you liked about the book and why you would recommend it. Your review doesn't have to be fancy, or long, just honest and positive. Then, post that review anywhere you think it might be helpful, beginning of course with Amazon. Thank you in advance for your review.

*Walter*

www.ingramcontent.com/pod-product-compliance
Lightning Source LLC
LaVergne TN
LVHW051014080826
845145LV00009B/2620

* 9 7 8 1 7 3 4 6 7 5 0 8 5 *